# POCKET
# ENCOURAGER

## *for* *Men*

# POCKET ENCOURAGER
## *for Men*

*Biblical Help for Difficult Times*

By Selwyn Hughes
with contributions from
Dr Bill and Frances Munro
David and Maureen Brown
Keith Tondeur
Hilary Vogel

*May our*
*Lord Jesus Christ himself*
*and God our Father,*
*who loved us and by his grace*
*gave us eternal encouragement*
*and good hope,*
*encourage your hearts*
*and strengthen you*
*in every good deed and word.*

*2 Thessalonians 2:16–17*

*Pocket Encourager for Men*

Copyright © CWR 2001

ISBN 1 85345 177 0

Concept development, editing, design and production by CWR

Printed by Linney Print, Mansfield

Published by CWR, Waverley Abbey House, Waverley Lane,
Farnham, Surrey GU9 8EP

# Contents

1   When You Just Can't Stop

2   When God Seems Far Away

3   When You Get the Blame

4   When Fear Transcends

5   When You Struggle to Do It All Yourself

6   When Facing Loneliness

7   When Things Get Too Much

8   When Forgiving is Not Easy

9   When You Need Help Making the Right Choice

10   When You No Longer Want to Pray

11   When You Need to Manage Your Life Better

12   When Doubts Crowd In

13   When You Experience Wrong Thoughts

14   When Dealing with Failure

15   When You Need Cheering Up

16   When Hopes are Dashed

17   When You End Up Working 7 Days a Week

18   When You Fall into Grievous Sin

19   When Your Security is Shaken

20   When the Stress Gets Too Much

21     When Trusting is Hard

22     When Coping with Depression

23     When Your Marriage is Shaken 1

24     When Your Marriage is Shaken 2

25     When You Doubt that God is Good

26     When Caring for Others

27     When Facing Bitter Disappointment

28     When Counting the Cost of Discipleship

29     When You Need Divine Guidance

30     When the Storm Rages

31     When You Feel Forgotten by God

32     When Facing Redundancy

33     When Caught in Debt

34     When Struggling with Anger

35     When Battling with Sexual Frustration

36     When God's Promises are Delayed

37     When Your Love for the Lord Begins to Wane

38     When Marriage Fails

39     When Someone Close to You Dies

40     When Sick and Tired of Being Sick and Tired

# Everyone needs
# *Encouragement*

There's nothing sentimental about encouragement. In all the years I have been a counsellor I have met only a few people who didn't respond positively to a few carefully chosen, biblically-based words of support. Some of the most remembered moments in my own life have been when I have been overtaken by a pressing problem and someone has come alongside and stimulated my faith with a God-given, reassuring word.

The word discourage means "to deprive of courage, to dishearten, to deter". Almost every day we face discouraging circumstances and situations: a put-down from someone, a critical word, plans that don't seem to work out, loneliness, sorrow, failure or doubts. In contrast, the word encourage means "to inspire with new confidence and courage, to give spirit or hope, to hearten, to spur on, to give help." It is gratifying when we are caught up in the throes of discouragement to have a friend, relative or colleague come alongside and say something (or does something) that is encouraging. But what do we do when such encouragement is not available?

That famous Old Testament character David was once in this situation. The incident is recorded for us in the First Book of Samuel chapters 27, 29 and 30. Fleeing for his life from King Saul, David offered his services, and those of his 600 men, to King Achish, a Philistine. And the king, accepting the offer, gave David and his men first Gath, then the city of Ziklag for their home. David, his men and their families settled there.

One day King Achish took his troops to join in a combined Philistine attack against Israel, and astonishingly, David and his soldiers went along with them to fight against their own people. But King Achish's colleagues refused to trust David and his men in a battle against their own, so they decided to send them back to Ziklag. On returning there they found that a group of desert raiders called the Amalekites had burned the city to the ground and had taken captive everyone they had found. David and his men, we read: "wept aloud until they had no strength left to weep" (1 Samuel 30:4).

To make matters worse, David's men turned on him and blamed him for their predicament. They even discussed among themselves the idea of stoning him: "each one was bitter in spirit because of his sons and daughters" (1 Samuel 30:6). In addition to these problems David also had to cope with the loss of his own family. His state of distress was such that right there his career could easily have come to an end. Then we are introduced to one of the great "buts" of the Bible: "But David encouraged ... himself in the Lord his God" (v.6, Amplified Bible).

How did he do it? He would have prayed of course, and that is always important when dealing with discouragement. But I think he did something more – he recalled what he knew of God, and thought about what he had learned concerning the Almighty as a shepherd boy when he meditated upon Him in the Judean hills.

"The secret of recovering your footing spiritually" says Jim Packer, the well-known theologian, "lies in the little word *think*". That was undoubtedly where David began; he made himself recall what he knew of God and applied it to his own situation at that moment. The Puritans used to call it "preaching to oneself". Every time we are discouraged, every time we reel under the blow of some traumatic experience, every time our feelings scream out in pain, we must assert the facts of our faith over our feelings. We can't wait for the unpleasant and uncomfortable feelings to subside; we must take control over the runaway feelings by reminding ourselves of what we know about God.

I imagine that David would have reminded himself of such facts as these: God is sovereign, God is love, God is forgiving, God is faithful, God is consistent, God is merciful. Dwelling on these thoughts would have brought great encouragement to David's heart. The consequence of all this was that he found the guidance he needed to restore the situation completely. Read the story for yourself in the rest of 1 Samuel 30.

Every Christian man ought to know how to do what David did, and this pocketbook is an attempt to help you to do just that. Friends and family are great (thank God for them), but we must know how to think biblically about life's problems, to talk to ourselves about the facts of our faith and then find the appropriate scriptures that relate to our problem.

It is essential to know what parts of the Bible to turn to in times of testing, and to know also how to talk ourselves into a new mood of optimism and faith. The things we tell ourselves greatly affect the way we feel – and this is why we must learn to fill our minds with the truths of God's eternal and unchanging Word.

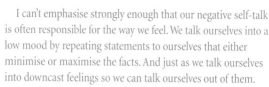

I can't emphasise strongly enough that our negative self-talk is often responsible for the way we feel. We talk ourselves into a low mood by repeating statements to ourselves that either minimise or maximise the facts. And just as we talk ourselves into downcast feelings so we can talk ourselves out of them.

As a Christian counsellor I have often asked people the question "What discourages you?'" In this publication we have taken key issues addressed in the earlier CWR publication *Your Personal Encourager*, and added further subjects from other authors who are involved in the "ministry of encouragement" and which are particularly relevant to men. If a particular problem that you are facing does not fall within these categories then look for the one that comes closest to it. I feel confident you will find something that will revive, refresh and minister to your spirit.

This Pocket Encourager can be used in two ways. One, to help you find a relevant scripture and thoughts you need to consider when overtaken by some aspect of discouragement, and two, as a foundation from which you can minister to others whenever they need encouragement.

It goes without saying that the power of this publication lies in the key words of Scripture which it highlights. In every instance prayer is vital and should be based on Scripture and built around such great themes as God's sovereignty, power, compassion, forgiveness – the same truths that David would undoubtedly have reflected on in those discouraging moments at Ziklag. The thoughts and ideas recorded here have been used in countless counselling situations over the years. Many people have told me they have found them helpful. I hope you will too.

Encouragement must not be regarded as mere sentimentality. We should realise Scripture is equally encouraging when it confronts and challenges us as it is when it consoles and comforts us. To be faced with a challenge when we are hurting may not be what we most want, but it may be what we most need. An African tribe says of medicine that is not too pleasing to the taste but does them good: "It hurts better." Keep in mind that when God challenges us it is only that we might be brought to the place of complete and utter dependency upon Him. God not only lifts the standards to great heights, but also provides the power to reach up to them.

Personally, I find it deeply encouraging that God thinks so much of me that He will not let me get away with things that damage my potential and hinder my effectiveness for Him. *He loves me as I am but He loves me too much to let me stay as I am.* So remember it is still the ministry of encouragement that is at work when Scripture speaks to us in a challenging and confronting way. See these as the Lord's "loving reproofs", for that is just what they are.

May you, like David at Ziklag, learn the skill of encouraging yourself and others in the Lord your God.

*Selwyn Hughes*

Selwyn Hughes,
Waverley Abbey House, Farnham, Surrey, England.

# POCKET
# ENCOURAGER

## *for* *Men*

# When You Just Can't
# *Stop*

A few years ago, a heart clinic in America noticed that many of the chairs in their waiting room were getting worn out along the front edge. They started to observe patients in the waiting room and found that many of them sat right on the edge of their chairs, hence the wear and tear on this part of the chairs. This led them to look more deeply into the behaviour of their heart patients.

They found that such people live in the fast lane; drive fast, eat fast, talk fast. Not for them a relaxing holiday on the beach. They go scuba diving or hang gliding or hire a car and visit all things of interest in a 50-mile radius. They feel guilty doing nothing. They are often workaholics and can be very ambitious, not just for themselves, but for their ministry, organisation or church.

There is nothing wrong with using time profitably or working hard, within reason. But there is bound to be wear and tear on the individual who is overdoing it.

The Lord Jesus was the most balanced man who ever

lived. He was not under time pressures.
Despite all the demands on Him,
He had time to spend with His
Father, with His disciples, and
alone. He preached to large
crowds but had time to stop and
speak to individuals. Is there a lesson
here for you?

*"He who kneels
the most
stands best."*
D.L. Moody

### Bible Verses to Help You
*Be still, and know that I am God.*
*(Psalm 46:10)*

*Cast all your anxiety on Him because He cares for you.*
*(1 Peter 5:7)*

### Suggested further reading
*Philippians 4:1–9*

### Reflect and respond
Are you driven?

Do you need to, "let go and let God"?

Should you be spending more time with the Lord, listening
to Him?

# When God Seems Far *Away*

Sometimes even mature Christians who have followed the Lord for many years go through times when God seems very far away. In the main there are three possible reasons for this.

First, the problem can stem from a purely physical cause. Sickness, stress or overwork can affect our moods to such a degree that we think we are spiritually low when the real problem lies in a poor physical condition. This is why God gave Elijah a period of rest and recuperation (see 1 Kings 19).

Second, God might seem far away because of sin. God has so built our spiritual system that when we sin, conviction descends. In this situation repentance is the only way back. Repentance, remember, means more than just "being sorry"; it means being sorry enough to quit. When repentance has taken effect we can be sure that our relationship with God will be restored.

The third reason – and by far the most common one – for feeling that God is far away, is because we fail to take the time to maintain our relationship with Him. If we don't take the time to talk to God regularly in prayer and listen to Him through reading His Word, then ought it to surprise us that the relationship between us and Him begins to deteriorate? As someone put it: "if God seems far away – guess who moved?" God never moves away from us – it's we who move away from Him.

> *"Thou hast made us for Thyself, O Lord; and our heart is restless until it rests in Thee."*
> *St Augustine*

### Bible Verses to Help You
*God has said, "Never will I leave you; never will I forsake you."*
*(Hebrews 13:5b)*

*"God did this so that men would seek him and perhaps reach out for him and find him, though he is not far from each one of us. 'For in him we live and move and have our being.'"*
*(Acts 17:27–28)*

### Suggested further reading
Psalm 139:7–10

### Reflect and respond
Do you need a physical health check-up?

Have you dealt with any unresolved sin?

Have you spent quality time with God lately?

# *When You Get the*
# *Blame*

We live in a culture of blame. Always the cry is Whose fault is it? Who was to blame? Who should be punished? Graffiti on a Chicago subway stated, Humpty Dumpty was pushed. Manufacturers and accident insurers in the USA are so afraid of being sued, that they go to extreme lengths to try to protect themselves. The cry is, Someone should pay for this.

Studies have shown that the more a victim blames another person for the accident, the more poorly he copes. Anger and bitterness can go on for years. Being unforgiving, angry, resentful and bitter is wrong in God's eyes, but it can also damage our minds and bodies and delay recovery. We teach to forgive and not to harbour bitterness. "Get rid of all bitterness, rage and anger, brawling and slander, along with every form of malice. Be kind and compassionate to one another, forgiving each other, just as in Christ God forgave you" (Ephesians 4:31–32). It may be difficult, almost impossible to do in our own strength, and often we will need God's help and grace to do it, but do it we must if we do not want to be damaged ourselves.

Even more important, we must forgive so that we may be forgiven. "And when you stand praying, if you hold anything against anyone, forgive him, so that your Father in heaven may forgive you your sins" (Mark 11:25).

*Deal with the faults of others as gently as with your own.*
Chinese Proverb

### Bible Verses to Help You
*Resentment kills a fool …*
*(Job 5:2)*

*Be kind and compassionate to one another, forgiving each other, just as in Christ God forgave you.*
*(Ephesians 4:32)*

### Suggested further reading
Colossians 3:1–15; 1 Corinthians 13:5

### Reflect and respond
Are you harbouring resentment or a grudge?

Is there someone you need to forgive?

Love keeps no record of wrongs – look to put right any wrongs this week.

# *When Fear*
# *Transcends*

Fear, it must be said at once, can be a friend as well as a foe. A healthy fear keeps us from rushing across a traffic-infested street, it compels caution and preserves life. An unhealthy fear, however, can quickly enslave the whole personality.

How does Christ enable His children to deal with fear? He does it by imparting to us the energy and power to face anything that comes, assuring us that whatever the difficulties we have to face, we can be more than a match for them, in Him. The apostle Paul puts it like this: "For God did not give us a spirit of timidity, but a spirit of power, of love and of self-discipline" (2 Timothy 1:7).

The one thing that underlies all unhealthy fear is the desire for avoidance. The fearful heart says: "When afraid – avoid." The Holy Spirit, however, enables us to face whatever it is that troubles us, knowing that no matter what happens it can never separate us from God and His unending love. The apostle John says, "Perfect love drives out fear" (1 John 4:18). Resting in His love – a love that will never let us go – we can move into any situation that makes us afraid with a confidence that transcends all fear. Fear says: "Avoid." Faith says, "Confront." Therefore move with God towards the thing you fear and just see what God will do.

> *"Faith is not a sword just to grab ... faith is a way of life. Feed your faith and starve your doubts to death!"*
>
> Lester Sumrall

### Bible Verses to Help You

*Even though I walk through the valley of the shadow of death, I will fear no evil, for you are with me; your rod and your staff, they comfort me.*
*(Psalm 23:4)*

*The Lord is my light and my salvation – whom shall I fear?*
*(Psalm 27:1)*

### Suggested further reading

Psalm 46:1–2

### Reflect and respond

Is your fear a godly or worldly fear?

Have you strengthened your spirit with the Word?

Have you been avoiding rather than confronting your fear?

# *When You Struggle to Do It All*
## *Yourself*

Are you bad at delegating? Delegating is one way of releasing others into their gifting, and reducing your stress. In Exodus 18, Jethro, Moses father-in-law, was aware that Moses was taking on too much and was getting stressed. Jethro's advice was that Moses should appoint other judges and delegate much of the work to them. So delegation is a God-honoured principle.

There are many reasons why you may not want to delegate: I'm in charge around here so I need to do it myself; I would do it better myself; I would feel guilty for imposing this on others; Maybe the one I delegate to will do it better than I could, and I may go down in others' estimation (Perish the thought!); If I don't do it, nobody else will do it and it probably won't be done, but people expect me to do it.

None of the reasons usually given should be sufficient to deflect you from taking the necessary actions. Yes, it may take longer. But this is an investment of time not a waste of it. Yes, others may not do it as well but at least it will be done. And even if it is not perfect, it will probably be good enough.

*Together Everyone Achieves More.*

Moses had to be brave enough to delegate. Are you? It might make a difference as to whether you survive or not!

### Bible Verses to Help You

*The Lord said to Moses: " Bring me seventy of Israel's elders ... They will help you carry the burden of the people so that you will not have to carry it alone."*
(Numbers 11:16–17)

*It was he who gave some to be apostles, some to be prophets, some to be evangelists, and some to be pastors and teachers ..."*
(Ephesians 4:11)

### Suggested further reading
Romans 12:1–8

### Reflect and respond
Should you be delegating some of your tasks?

Are there more important tasks you could be doing with your time?

Are you doing what you do best and allowing others to do likewise?

# When Facing
# *Loneliness*

Loneliness often arises from circumstances beyond our control (when we are shut in by sickness or disability, for example). But loneliness can also come from an inability to relate well to others. When we are lonely because of life's circumstances we must never forget that nothing can interfere with our communion with heaven. Shut off from others we can still have contact with the Friend of friends – Jesus

Many people, though, are lonely not by reason of their circumstances but because of an inability to relate. In a needy world like ours, it has been said, anyone can have friendship who will give friendship. A very lonely individual became someone who was sought after by many after he heard his pastor say in a sermon, "The best way to have a friend is to be a friend." He went home, got down on his knees and prayed, "Lord, forgive me for focusing more on myself than others. From now on I will move towards others with the same love by which You move towards me." As his thoughts changed from self-centredness to other-centredness he became a more interesting and attractive personality. His circle of friends widened and he became outgoing in all his relationships.

*The best way to have a friend is to be a friend.*

No Christian is ever without the friendship of God, but when lacking the friendship of human beings, keep in mind that when we give ourselves to others they will often give themselves to us.

### *Bible Verses to Help You*
*Then you will call, and the Lord will answer; you will cry for help, and he will say: Here am I.*
*(Isaiah 58:9)*

*Come near to God and he will come near to you.*
*(James 4:8)*

### *Suggested further reading*
Psalm 139:1–18

### *Reflect and respond*
Have you drawn close to your heavenly Friend – Jesus?

Have you made yourself a friend to others?

Could you do more to focus on others rather than yourself?

# When Things Get
# *Too Much*

Have you felt like getting away to a desert island, wanting the pain of the pressure to stop? Sometimes it seems as though there is no way out. A loved one dies. We may be deserted by a wife or husband. A relationship is broken off, or the church is in turmoil. Intractable situations like these can be very stressful but you must beware the quick fix. There may be short term gains, but long term consequences.

If you are in a difficult time, take time to pray and ask God's guidance for your next move. It may be that God wants you to go through the testing time. He may want you to learn something specific, to refine you, to enrich you or simply to teach you to become more dependent on Him. If you immediately take things into your own hands you may miss God's opportunity and plan for you.

God has said, "Fear not, for I have redeemed you; I have summoned you by name; you are mine. When you pass through the waters, I will be with you; and when you pass through the rivers, they will not sweep over you. When

you walk through the fire, you will not be burned;
the flames will not set you ablaze.
For I am the Lord, your God, the
Holy One of Israel, your
Saviour" (Isaiah 43:1–3). So be
encouraged. The darkest time is
often just before the dawn.

> *"He can give
> only according to
> His might; therefore
> He always gives more
> than we ask for."*
> *Martin Luther*

### Bible Verses to Help You
*Blessed is the man who perseveres under trial, because
when he has stood the test, he will receive the crown of life
that God has promised to those who love him.*
*(James 1:12)*

*The name of the Lord is a strong tower; the righteous run
to it and are safe.*
*(Proverbs 18:10)*

### Suggested further reading
1 Corinthians 10:1–13

### Reflect and respond
Are you tempted to sell the future to purchase the present?

Perhaps God wants you to go through the current pressures
– talk to Him about it.

# *When Forgiving*
# *is Not Easy*

S ome think Christianity sets an impossible standard
when it calls on believers to forgive all those who
have hurt or injured them. But with God "all things are
possible". There are three main reasons why we may find
it difficult to forgive.

First, we do not have a sufficiently deep realisation of
how much we ourselves have been forgiven. The sin of
another against us is as nothing when compared to our
sin against God – yet He has forgiven us.

Second, holding resentment or indignation against
another who has hurt us gives us a sense of power and
control over them, and when we give it up, we are left
feeling somewhat helpless. But it is to helplessness we are
called in the words: "'It is mine to avenge, I will repay,'
says the Lord" (Romans 12:19). Forgiveness involves
giving up control and trusting God with the outcome.

A third reason is what we might call "misplaced
dependency". This occurs when we move from dependency on God to dependency on others. Then when they
hurt us, we stumble because we believe we need them in

order to function. This is why we are always hurt most by those who are closest to us.

Forgiveness, we must remember, is not so much a feeling but a decision – an action of the will. You decide to forgive, whether you feel like it or not. You supply the willingness, God will supply the power.

> *"The greatest single cause of atheism in the world today is Christians who acknowledge Jesus with their lips, then walk out the door and deny Him by their lifestyle."*
> *Brennan Manning*

### Bible Verses to Help You
*Bear with each other and forgive whatever grievances you may have against one another. Forgive as the Lord forgave you.*
*(Colossians 3:13)*

*… as far as the east is from the west, so far has he removed our transgressions from us.*
*(Psalm 103:12)*

### Suggested further reading
2 Corinthians 2:8–11

### Reflect and respond
Do you feel overwhelmed with your unforgiveness? Go to the Father with your problem.

Have you made the decision to forgive?

# When You Need Help Making *the* Right Choice

U nless we have a clear idea of what our priorities should be, we will always be left wondering, "Did I make the right choice?".

I believe that God has an order of priorities for us. If we go by His order we will please Him, we have His authority and things will go well for us. I believe the order is God, our spouse, our children, parents and family, church, good works, personal interests. Some of these categories may not apply to you, you can leave them out. You may want to add others of your own like friends.

Priority does not mean necessarily more time spent. We may spend more time at work, but this does not mean it has top priority. God demands first place – your relationship with Him is what is most important. What you do for others comes out of that. When conflicting demands come it is wonderful to be able to fall back on this order of priorities to guide us, knowing that it has God's authority. Although it is sometimes difficult to be brave enough to follow the order, the price is worth paying.

It is important, too, that even when different demands are not being made on us, we keep to God's order. This is how He has made us, and our lives to function. If we do not, then there can be long-term consequences.

*"I have so much to do that I spend several hours in prayer before I am able to do it."*

*John Wesley*

### Bible Verses to Help You

**"*Those who honour me I will honour …*"**
*(1 Samuel 2:30 )*

**"But as for me and my household, we will serve the Lord."**
*(Joshua 24:15)*

### Suggested further reading

Ephesians 3:1–10

### Reflect and respond

Have you worked out with God's help what God's priorities are in your life? (What would you least like to lose?)

Do you need to re-order your life to bring it into line with God's order?

# When You No Longer Want to *Pray*

The obstacles to prayer are many. Some claim they don't have time to pray, others that they have no place to pray. Well, it's always possible to go for a walk with Jesus. Still others complain they don't know what to pray for. Then make a list – friends and loved ones who need to be converted, those known to you who are sick, the needs of the church you attend, your own needs, and so on.

By far the most common obstacle to prayer, however, is disinclination. People do not pray because they do not feel like it. But we must not assume that prayer is effective only when it arises from an eager and emotional heart. Those who have achieved great power in prayer tell us that floods of feeling come only now and again in their times of intercession. If we have an appointment to meet someone whom we regard as important, do we break it a few moments before the meeting because we feel disinclined? Common courtesy tells us it would not be right. Are we to be less courteous with God?

The great practitioners of prayer assure us God can do

more with us when we pray against our inclination than when we pray with it. The willingness to submit to Him deepens our surrender; our resolve to go to God builds steel into our Christian commitment. It is faith, not feeling, that measures the efficacy of prayer.

> *"Intercessory prayer might be defined as loving our neighbour on our knees."*
> Charles Brent

### Bible Verses to Help You
*And pray in the Spirit on all occasions with all kinds of prayers and requests. With this in mind, be alert and always keep on praying for all the saints.*
(Ephesians 6:18)

*I cry aloud to the Lord; I lift up my voice to the Lord for mercy. I pour out my complaint before him; before him I tell my trouble.*
(Psalm 142:1–2)

### Suggested further reading
Psalm 42:5–11

### Reflect and respond
Are you always making excuses not to pray?

Have you persevered above your feelings?

Submit your prayers to God in faith – just do it!

# *When You Need to Manage Your Life* **Better**

**1.** Stop doing some of the things you are doing. Preferably the non-essential, least important. Experts in time management tell us that we spend 80% of our time on the 20% least important things. Do you really need to do all you are doing?

**2.** Stop taking on any more, at least before you have thought about it and prayed about it. Jesus, with all the pressures and demands on Him, did not try to do everything and sometimes said No.

**3.** If deadlines are a problem, try to leave yourself more time. We hear much about rushing for trains and planes nowadays and meeting deadlines. But we hear little about start times. When possible, try to start earlier for the train or plane, or on the journey, or on the assignment. Then you may not be so rushed.

**4.** Try to develop greater efficiency. This may mean an investment in time – of learning better ways, or of developing time-saving systems.

**5.** Would you rather be effective or efficient? There is little point in being super-efficient if what you do is not effective. Being effective is doing the right thing.

**6.** Plan. If you fail to plan you are planning to fail. It is especially important to plan in the important, but not necessarily urgent, things – like time with God, with your spouse, your children, friends, building relationships.

*"God loves us the way we are but He loves us too much to leave us that way."*
Leighton Ford

### Bible Verses to Help You
*... and the wise heart will know the proper time and procedure. For there is a proper time and procedure for every matter ...*
(Ecclesiastes 8:5–6)

*"For I know the plans I have for you," declares the Lord, "plans to prosper you and not to harm you, plans to give you hope and a future."*
(Jeremiah 29:11)

### Suggested further reading
James 1:2–8

### Reflect and respond
The time you have each day is given to you by God.

Are you being a good steward of your time? Have you prayed about this?

Should you be stopping certain things?

# When Doubts
## *Crowd In*

Many Christians feel that if doubt exists in their minds they cannot be true believers. This arises from a wrong understanding of the nature of doubt. "Doubt," says Os Guinness, "is a state of mind in suspension between faith and unbelief so that it is neither of them wholly, and it is each only partly. It is faith in two minds."

Perhaps we can better understand doubt by taking the analogy of fear. Many think fear is the opposite of courage, but it is not. The opposite of fear is cowardice. Fear is the half-way stage between the two. It is not wrong to feel fear in certain situations. The real question is what do we do with it – something courageous or something cowardly? It is the same with doubt. It stands undecided between faith and unbelief and has to choose between the two.

A man one day came to Jesus and confessed to his struggle with doubt (Mark 9:14–29). The struggle with doubt must be seen as a sign of faith, not unbelief.

*What destroys faith is not doubt but disobedience* – the

unwillingness to bring those doubts and lay them at the feet of Jesus. The prayer of the man in the incident referred to, "I do believe; help me overcome my unbelief!" is one that all of us must echo whenever we are caught in the throes of doubt. This attitude changes everything.

> *"Believe your beliefs and doubt your doubts."*
> F. F. Bosworth

### Bible Verses to Help You
*Then he said to Thomas, "Put your finger here; see my hands. Reach out your hand and put it into my side. Stop doubting and believe." Thomas said to him, "My Lord and my God!"*
(John 20:27–28)

*Immediately Jesus reached out his hand and caught him. "You of little faith," he said, "why did you doubt?"*
(Matthew 14:31)

### Suggested further reading
Job 42:1–5

### Reflect and respond
Stop mentally beating yourself up when you doubt.

Do you wallow in doubt, or use it as a springboard to faith?

Call upon God to deliver you from doubt.

# *When You Experience*
# *Wrong Thoughts*

What we hear, or read or watch can change our body chemistry and functioning and affect our feelings. If you watch an exciting film or sporting event on TV, the adrenaline can surge, your pulse race and you feel tense. Reading a newspaper account of a despicable murder, child abuse, or neglect, can make your blood boil, your blood pressure can go up and you feel that you might burst a blood vessel. Listening to a story of heroism or bravery, a child being saved, you can feel a lump in your throat.

Every day the TV brings right into our living rooms news of hate and terrorism and war from the Middle East, Africa, Europe. There are sickening reports on TV and in our newspapers of murder, rape, abuse, violence, burglary.

Perhaps there is little wonder that fed a diet of such things and given what we know about how they affect us, that we can experience thinking out of line with God's best. While TV can be educational and we should be aware of our world and how we can be salt and light, we should be aware of the effect our reading and viewing has on us.

We should take time to read God's Word (just for ourselves), listen to good music, and uplifting stories. In short, we should take St Paul's advice seriously about what we should be filling our minds with.

> "The inward area is the first place of loss of true Christian life, of true spirituality, and the outward sinful act is the result."
> Francis Schaeffer

### Bible Verses to Help You

*Whatever is true ... noble ... right ... pure ... lovely ... admirable – if anything is excellent or praiseworthy – think about such things.*
*(Philippians 4:8)*

*For as [a man] thinks within himself, so he is.*
*(Proverbs 23:7 NIV footnote)*

### Suggested further reading

Romans 12:2

### Reflect and respond

Is your daily reading and viewing uplifting?

Do you need to change the balance – choose to fill your mind with that which is holy.

Do you lend an ear to gossip?

# 14

# *When Dealing with*
## *Failure*

It's hard to look objectively at things when one has failed. When Millais first exhibited his "Ophelia" in 1852 one critic dubbed it "O Failure!" It is said that Millais was plagued by these words for the rest of his life.

When overtaken by failure sit down as soon as possible and prayerfully begin to analyse the reason for the failure. Consider the possibility that God may have allowed this failure because it was part of His purpose for your life. Many have discovered that God allowed failure in their life to turn their thoughts in a new direction of service for Him.

If, however, after prayer and careful consideration of this possibility you are sure you have God's approval for continuing along the same lines, then ask yourself, Have I contributed to this failure by wrong timing, failure to weigh up the pros and cons, disregard of moral principles, insensitivity to other people's feelings ... and so on? Having learned the lessons that come from failure – try again.

A Christian poster I once saw showed a man in a Tshirt with the admission "I gave up". In the corner of the poster, barely visible, was a drawing of a little black hill and on it a very tiny cross. These words were printed beneath it: "I didn't". The One who triumphed over all obstacles holds out His hands to you. Take His hand and if another purpose has not been shown you – try again.

> *"The worst is not to fail, but to give up."*
> Ed Cole

### Bible Verses to Help You
*If the Lord delights in a man's way, he makes his steps firm; though he stumble, he will not fall, for the Lord upholds him with his hand.*
*(Psalm 37:23–24)*

*I press on towards the goal to win the prize for which God has called me heavenwards in Christ Jesus.*
*(Philippians 3:14)*

### Suggested further reading
Proverbs 3:1–5

### Reflect and respond
Are your goals God's goals?

Have you taken responsibility for your own actions?

Trust God to deliver you in your circumstances.

# 15

# When You Need
## *Cheering Up*

Did you know that laughter reduces stress levels, and is good for our emotional, mental and physical health too. Norman Cousins was suffering from cancer. He believed that if he laughed enough, the chemical and hormonal changes in his body could cure his cancer. He bought and rented as many comedy films that he could get hold of and watched them and laughed for hours on end. Sure enough, his cancer was cured.

In a recent study, two groups of people were given very intricate problems to solve. But before they attempted the problems, one group was asked to watch a quite harrowing documentary video, while the other watched a comedy film. The group who had watched the comedy performed much better at the problem solving than the group who had watched the documentary.

God Himself is the primary source of our joy, and we will experience this as a fruit of the Spirit (Galatians 5:22), and 1 Thessalonians 1:6 states, "... in spite of severe suffering, you welcomed the message with the joy given by the Holy Spirit". The Bible reveals that we can receive joy directly from God Himself. "May the God of hope fill you with all joy and peace as you trust in him, so that you may overflow with hope by the power of the Holy Spirit" (Romans 15:13). The Father loves to see His children full of joy.

*"I guess a man is about as cheerful as he decides to be."*

*Abraham Lincoln*

So go on, have a good laugh!

### Bible Verses to Help You

*A cheerful heart is good medicine …*
*(Proverbs 17:22)*

*Our mouths were filled with laughter, our tongues with songs of joy. Then it was said among the nations, "The Lord has done great things for them."*
*(Psalm 126:2)*

### Suggested further reading

Galatians 5:22

### Reflect and respond

Where are you seeking to find your joy?

A cheerful look brings joy to the heart (Proverbs 15:30). Do you need to lighten up a bit – should you be smiling more?

Be filled with the Spirit. (Ephesians 5:18)

# 16

# When Hopes are
# *Dashed*

Hope is one of the cardinal values of the Christian faith. "And now these three remain", said the apostle Paul in 1 Corinthians 13:13, "faith, hope and love". All through the New Testament, hope is spoken of in the highest terms.

We must differentiate, however, between the word "hope" as it is used in Scripture and the way it is used in ordinary conversation. Sometimes people say, "I hope things will get better", or "I am hoping for an increase in my salary", but we are not given any guarantees in Scripture that everything we "hope" for in this sense will come our way. When the Bible talks about "hope" it is talking about the certainty we have as Christians that God's eternal purposes will never be thwarted. The thing that gives a Christian what the writer to the Hebrews calls a hope "both sure and steadfast" (Hebrews 6:19, AV) is the fact that God is on the throne. Have you noticed in the Scriptures that whenever God's servants were in trouble they were given a vision of the eternal throne? Isaiah ... David ... Ezekiel ... the apostle John. Why a throne? Because God rules from His throne, and no matter if appearances are to the contrary, He is always in control. The hope (or certainty) that God's purposes continue even if ours get pushed aside acts as an anchor to the soul. We must never forget it.

> *"Fulfilment of your destiny does not come in a moment, a month, or a year, but over a lifetime."*
> Casey Treat

### Bible Verses to Help You
*We have this hope as an anchor for the soul, firm and secure. It enters the inner sanctuary behind the curtain ...*
*(Hebrews 6:19)*

*Know therefore that the Lord your God is God; he is the faithful God, keeping his covenant of love to a thousand generations of those who love him and keep his commands.*
*(Deuteronomy 7:9)*

### Suggested further reading
Hebrews 11

### Reflect and respond
Is your hope in God or mere speculation?

Have you allowed His Word to fuel your hope?

Trust the Father, and watch your hope soar.

# 17

# When You End Up Working
## *7 Days a Week*

In the busiest week the universe has ever seen, God rested on the seventh day. He did not have to rest. He does not get tired. He never sleeps. Moreover, being an all-powerful God, He did not need to take six days to do His creation work. He could have done it all in the twinkling of an eye, Why then did He take so long and why did He rest? He did it as a pattern for us to follow.

Many of the cases of burnout or stress are caused by working seven days each week. You may find it difficult to do nothing. You may even feel guilty. There are many excuses why you must be busy seven days in the week. It takes courage to stop at least one day but my experience, and that of others who do, has been that, surprise, surprise, we are better able to cope during the rest of the week and miraculously all gets done that needs to be done in the other six days.

You need to be inventive to fit in with your own situation. You may have to work difficult hours. You need a day of rest in the week over and above the time needed for

gardening, DIY, housework and hobbies.
I believe this is how God has
made us to function. He knows
we need the rest. You may
ignore this, but there may be a
price to pay.

> *"God respects me when
> I work, but he loves me
> when I sing."*
> *Sir Rabindranath Tagore*

### Bible Verses to Help You
*By the seventh day God had finished the work he had been
doing; so on the seventh day he rested from all his work.*
*(Genesis 2:2)*

*There is a time for everything, and a season for every
activity under heaven.*
*(Ecclesiastes 3:1)*

### Suggested further reading
Genesis 2:1–10

### Reflect and respond
Are you having at least one day of rest in the week?

Are you brave enough to obey?

You will be blessed by the Lord for honouring Him.

# 18

# When You Fall Into
# *Grievous Sin*

Sin, it has been said, is not so much the breaking of God's laws as the breaking of His heart. How then do we relieve the hurt that lies upon the heart of God when we have fallen into grievous sin?

First, we must not minimise the sin. Nowadays there is a tendency to describe a moral mishap as just a "little" thing, or "it wasn't important". Cancer in the stomach is still cancer even though a person may pass off their discomfort as "a bit of indigestion". We don't make a deadly thing innocuous by giving it a different name.

Second, we must confess the sin to God. We must cry out to Him as did the psalmist, "Have mercy on me, O God, according to your unfailing love ... blot out my transgressions. Wash away all my iniquity and cleanse me from my sin" (Psalm 51:1–2).

Third, if the sin has involved others then we must seek to put things right with them also. It is always helpful to discuss this matter with a minister or a Christian counsellor, however, before embarking on a course of action so as to avoid unnecessary complications.

Fourth, we must walk into the future clean and more dependent than ever on God's empowering grace. All the resources of heaven are engaged against sin, and the reason why we fall into it is because we do not avail ourselves of those resources.

> "Get alone with Jesus –
> and either tell Him that
> you do not want sin to
> die out in you – or else
> tell Him that at all costs
> you want to be identified
> with His death."
> *Oswald Chambers*

### Bible Verses to Help You

*If we confess our sins, he is faithful and just and will forgive us our sins and purify us from all unrighteousness.*
(1 John 1:9)

*Blessed is he whose transgressions are forgiven, whose sins are covered. Blessed is the man whose sin the Lord does not count against him and in whose spirit is no deceit.*
(Psalm 32:1–2)

### Suggested further reading
James 4:6–10

### Reflect and respond
Have you taken responsibility for your sin?

Have you confessed your sin and settled things with others?

Look to your future with a clean heart and lean upon His grace.

# 19

# When Your Security is
# *Shaken*

The stressor that affects more people than any other, and causes most stress, is insecurity or uncertainty. When you feel secure you can relax, and get on with your life. But if you feel insecure, you can become anxious, worried, fearful and stressed about the future. You will probably find it difficult to make decisions.

Many people depend on their position or ministry for security, and if things go awry, security goes and anxiety and stress follow. Recently a large group of male and female civil servants who were in a department threatened with privatisation were compared with another group in a department where no threat existed. There was a marked deterioration in the health of the group under threat compared with the secure group.

You may depend on other things – your pension – then you hear of dishonesty or mismanagement in the pension funds and you begin to wonder, is mine safe?

Perhaps you have been depending on your church congregation for encouragement and support; but people are found to have feet of clay and you feel disillusioned and hurt.

Are you stressed because your security has been taken away, or is being threatened, or may be in the future? God is the answer, as He is to everything. He is the only person who is entirely dependable and has made us to find our security only in Him. If you put your trust in Him, you are guaranteed absolute security.

> "I have held many things in my hands, and I have lost them all; but whatever I have placed in God's hands, that I still possess."
> *Martin Luther.*

### Bible Verses to Help You

*My people have committed two sins: They have forsaken me, the spring of living water, and have dug their own cisterns, broken cisterns that cannot hold water.*
*(Jeremiah 2:13)*

*Some trust in chariots and some in horses, but we trust in the name of the Lord our God.*
*(Psalm 20:7)*

### Suggested further reading

Deuteronomy 33:20–27

### Reflect and respond

Do you feel insecure, fearful of the future – what are you depending on for your security?

Are these sources utterly dependable?

Only God is fully dependable. Are you building your life on the Rock?

# 20

# When the Stress Gets
# *Too Much*

Experts on stress tell us it comes from two main causes: too little change and too much change. Dr Thomas Holmes, a recognised authority on stress, measures it in terms of "units of change". The death of a loved one, for example, measures 100 units, a divorce 73 units, pregnancy 40 units, moving or refurbishing a home 25 units, and Christmas is given 12 units. His conclusion is that no one can handle more than 300 units of stress in a 12-month period without suffering physically or emotionally during the next two years.

The first thing to do when experiencing stress is to identify what is causing it. What is the trigger? What are the symptoms? What happened immediately prior to the symptoms occurring? (This can be a vital clue.) We must invite the Lord to help with the matter as we think and pray it through. Only when the cause is found can things be changed.

Next, we must consider why it is that we are victims of stress. Are we unable to move ahead because of fear, or are we going too fast because we are afraid of what we might discover about ourselves if we stopped? To the degree we lack security in God, to that degree we will be motivated to find it in something else. *The secure are less prone to stress because they already have what they want – inner peace of mind.*

> *"Oh, how great peace and quietness would he possess who should cut off all vain anxiety and place all his confidence in God."*
>
> Thomas à Kempis

### Bible Verses to Help You

*Take my yoke upon you and learn from me, for I am gentle and humble in heart, and you will find rest for your souls.*
(Matthew 11:29)

*Peace I leave with you; my peace I give you. I do not give to you as the world gives. Do not let your hearts be troubled and do not be afraid.*
(John 14:27)

### Suggested further reading

Psalm 139:1–7

### Reflect and respond

Have you identified what is causing your stress?

Have you included God in on the process of deliverance from stress?

Put your security in God today.

# 21

# When Trusting is
# *Hard*

Do you worry about tomorrow? Do you inwardly struggle to work out whether there will be enough money for food, clothes or enough preaching inspiration? And what about resources and help needed in the home?

Jesus teaches us in simple terms to trust Him one day at a time, and He will provide on that basis. We may sometimes feel as though we have suddenly run into a crisis, but God is never taken by surprise, He knows our needs better than we know ourselves, God's provision is, PRO (before) VISION (seeing), and it is very reassuring to know that He sees our needs in advance.

In Luke 12, starting at verse 22, Jesus says, "Do not worry about your life, what you will eat; or about your body, what you will wear. Life is more than food, and the body more than clothes ... Consider how the lilies grow. They do not labour or spin. Yet I tell you, not even Solomon in all his splendour was dressed like one of these. If that is how God clothes the grass of the field, which is here today, and tomorrow is thrown into the fire, how much more will he clothe you, O you of little faith."

Let us take this opportunity to open up ourselves to new areas of trust, and experience a greater dependency on God. By this we can know a greater measure of His faithfulness and provision for our needs.

*God makes a promise; faith believes it, hope anticipates it, patience quietly awaits it.*

### Bible Verses to Help You

*Look at the birds of the air; they do not sow or reap or store away in barns, and yet your heavenly Father feeds them. Are you not much more valuable than they?*
*(Matthew 6:26–27)*

### Suggested further reading

Psalm 95:1–11

### Reflect and respond

If you feel fearful, don't be afraid to ask someone to pray with you.

Recite Psalm 23 each day for the next week.

# 22

# When Coping with
# *Depression*

Almost everyone, from time to time, will confess to feelings of depression, but usually these feelings quickly pass. When they continue for a few weeks, however, and become increasingly acute, then medical opinion should be sought, if only to ascertain whether or not the cause is physical.

Many things can plunge us into a low mood – uncertainty about the future, a breakdown in relationships, financial difficulties, ageing, lack of purpose, and so on. The common denominator, though, with deeply depressed feelings is a sense of loss. A vital clue also to understanding what plunges us into depression is found when we examine the relationship between what we are doing and the expected rewards. If our actions and behaviours do not, over a period of time, bring us the rewards we expect then we can become so discouraged that we sink into a low mood.

The best remedy for all non-biological depression is to gain a new perspective – to turn one's gaze from earth to heaven. The psalmist in Psalm 42 sees that there is a thirst inside him that no one can meet except God. When he looks to God for the satisfaction of that thirst (rather than others), his soul then rests on the hope that no matter what happens, he remains secure as a person. Understanding this, and constantly applying it in our lives, is the key to overcoming and remaining free from depression.

*Though I sit in darkness, the Lord will be my light.*
*Micah 7:8*

### Bible Verses to Help You
*Why are you downcast, O my soul? Why so disturbed within me? Put your hope in God, for I will yet praise him, my Saviour and my God.*
*(Psalm 42:5)*

*The Lord is close to the broken-hearted and saves those who are crushed in spirit.*
*(Psalm 34:18)*

### Suggested further reading
Psalm 32:1–7

### Reflect and respond
Is your depression medically related?

Is your gaze towards heaven or earth?

Thirst after God and regain your hope.

# 23

# When Your Marriage is
## *Shaken* 1

Many of England's majestic cathedrals are in need of expensive repair. Often the cause for this is from the vibrations caused by traffic which affects the very foundations. An external force, the vehicle traffic, has created internal problems. Before any remedial work can be carried out an inspection and rectification of the foundations are called for.

So it is with marriage. Often external forces act upon our relationship, causing damage and lasting harm. It is not the pressure upon us that causes the damage, but what we are standing on – rock or sand? Are you standing upon the rock of Jesus? Is your marriage based upon God and His Holy Word? The Hebrew words, *Yasad* and *Musad*, are translated as foundation. They are used where what is to be built upon them is to endure and last for many generations. What you put down as a foundation into your marriage will affect not just you, but also your children and your children's children, and even their children.

Such foundations need to be laid with care, and carefully chosen to withstand the pressures to be inflicted upon them. Within marriage we equally need to lay a

quality foundation with care – that can take any
storm that comes at you.

Some of the actions to take in
laying these foundations are:
Recognising the need to say sorry
and to act unselfishly;

Learning to communicate and express
your feelings;
Learn to trust each other and God.

> *"A successful
> marriage demands a
> divorce; a divorce from
> your own self-love."*
> Paul Frost

### Bible Verses to Help You
*Love is patient, love is kind. It does not envy, it does not
boast, it is not proud. It is not rude, it is not self-seeking, it
is not easily angered, it keeps no record of wrongs. Love
does not delight in evil but rejoices with the truth. It always
protects, always trusts, always hopes, always perseveres.
Love never fails.*
(1 Corinthians 13:4–8)

*The foundations were laid with large stones of good
quality …*
(1 Kings 7:10)

### Suggested further reading
Nehemiah 1:1–2

### Reflect and respond
Foundations can be beautiful and adorned. They can also
reflect the beauty of the finished work.

Read and meditate on Revelation 21:18–21.

# 24

# *When Your Marriage is*
# *Shaken 2*

Every marriage can hit problems. At such times it can help to refocus our thoughts if we reflect on what we actually did on our wedding day when we covenanted together in the presence of God (Genesis 2:24).

In the Bible the word covenant is taken from two Hebrew words, *karoth berith*, which means to cut a covenant. In the Old Testament the sacrifice was cut in two, and in the New Testament it was the body of Jesus that was cut by the nails and the spear. In marriage there is the need to cut something, perhaps the ties with home. On a wedding day the symbols of cutting, sacrifice and covenant are there for all to see if we look.

As the bride walks down the aisle she symbolises the sacrifice both families have made in bringing up their children. The groom stands at the front awaiting his bride to symbolise the day Jesus will receive His Bride (Revelation 22:17). The groom stands away from his family to symbolise he has left his father and mother – a cutting away. The bride is given away, again to symbolise a leaving. Rings are exchanged to symbolise a joining together. Cutting of the wedding cake is to symbolise the cutting of a covenant. The toast symbolises that one day those of us who are in Christ will lift up the cup and drink of the new wine with Jesus in heaven (Matthew 26:29).

*A deaf husband and a blind wife are always a happy couple.*
French Proverb

Whenever a marriage faces problems it is good to reflect on what was actually done on the wedding day.

### Bible Verses to Help You
*According to the word that I covenanted with you ...*
*(Haggai 2:5 NKJ)*

*The man said, "This is now bone of my bones and flesh of my flesh; she shall be called 'woman', for she was taken out of man." For this reason a man will leave his father and mother and be united to his wife, and they will become one flesh.*
*(Genesis 2:23–24)*

### Suggested further reading
Genesis 17:1–7

### Reflect and respond
Are you in a crisis because you have not realised what plans God had for you on your wedding day?

Are you resisting God in your life or marriage?

Ask God, in prayer, what plans He has for both of you.

# 25

# When You Doubt that God is Good

"The root of sin", said Oswald Chambers, "is the belief that God is not good." There are a multitude of circumstances and events we have to face in a fallen world that suggest God is not good – earthquakes, famines, storms and floods that wipe out whole communities, disease, and so on.

Before radar was invented, the art of navigation depended on the existence of fixed points. Mariners took their bearings not from a cloud or a floating spar but from the stars and from things that were solid, such as a headland or a lighthouse. If a seaman took a bearing and found he was off course he would not doubt the star or the headland – he would doubt himself.

We need to do the same whenever we find ourselves doubting that God is good. We must see to it that we are fixed to the things that are fixed. The cross is one of those things. It is the irrefutable proof that God is love. When we look around and consider the many situations that seem to give the lie to the fact that God is love, we must not pretend these matters do not cause us problems. Rather, we must set them all over against the one thing that is crystal clear – God's love as demonstrated for us on Calvary. A God who would do that for us simply must be Love. *At the foot of Calvary the ground is fixed*.

> *"In the maddening maze of things,*
> *And tossed by storm and flood,*
> *To one fixed trust my spirit clings:*
> *I know that God is good!"*
> John Greenleaf Whittier.

## Bible Verses to Help You

*"Why do you call me good?" Jesus answered. "No-one is good – except God alone."*
*(Mark 10:18)*

*For God so loved the world that he gave his one and only Son, that whoever believes in him shall not perish but have eternal life. For God did not send his Son into the world to condemn the world, but to save the world through him.*
*(John 3:16–17)*

## Suggested further reading

1 Peter 2:1  5

## Reflect and respond

Is your thinking grounded in the Scriptures?

Have you confused worldly circumstances with God's will?

Fix your eyes once again on Calvary and God's love displayed there.

# 26

# *When Caring for*
# *Others*

We are all called to care for others. The most well-known "caring" story is of the Good Samaritan. Obviously, ministering to others will benefit them. But, the great thing is, as long as you are serving out of God's gifting, you can benefit too: "Blessed is he who is kind to the needy" (Proverbs 14:21). "But when you give to the needy, do not let your left hand know what your right hand is doing, so that your giving may be in secret. Then your Father, who sees what is done in secret, will reward you" (Matthew 6:3).

If you have a leadership role in a busy church, you may already have a lot of responsibilities and you may have to be careful that you do not take on too many, because this can be stressful. If you are alone and do not have family responsibilities, you could perhaps adopt someone in your church.

You may live on your own and find it difficult to care for others. But there are ways. You can give directly, or to a charity, either time or money. You can write a letter of encouragement – it will also benefit you, especially if you undertake to write regularly. You can pray for others. After Job had prayed for his friends, the Lord made him prosperous again and gave him twice as much as he had before (Job 42:10).

*Don't let the things you can't do stop you from doing the things you can do.*
Bobbie-Jean Merck

Caring for and being responsible for others can benefit them – but you also!

### Bible Verses to Help You
*For even the Son of Man did not come to be served, but to serve, and to give his life as a ransom for many."*
(Mark 10:45)

*The entire law is summed up in a single command: "Love your neighbour as yourself."*
(Galatians 5:14)

### Suggested further reading
1 John 4:7–16

### Reflect and respond
In what ways are you best equipped to care for others?

Remember love never fails. Even if your love is rebuffed it is not wasted as it benefits the giver as well as the recipient.

Sowing seeds of care, will bring a harvest of blessing and friendship.

# 27

# *When Facing Bitter*
# *Disappointment*

Hardly any of us can go through life without experiencing on occasions the dampening effect of disappointment. A friend we hoped would come through for us lets us down, an event on which we pinned a great deal of hope fails to materialise, an important promise made to us is broken. Dealing with such disappointments is not easy. The following three principles, however, when followed and practised should help.

First, we must accept that what has happened has happened. When, in the effort to get away from the pain of disappointment, we pretend that something has not happened, or that it has happened in a different way, we deceive ourselves. Integrity requires that whatever is true, whatever is real, must be faced.

Second, we must acknowledge our feelings. If we feel hurt, angry, frustrated, or any other negative emotions, we must be willing to face them. Unacknowledged emotions invariably cause trouble.

Third, we must bring the issue to God in prayer,

remembering that He can take every one of life's disappointments and make them work for us rather than against us (see Romans 8:28–29). Just change the first letter of "Disappointment" from "D" to "H" and *"Disappointment"* becomes *"His-appointment"*.

*"Deep in unfathamable mines Of never failing skill He treasures up His bright designs And works His sovereign will."*
William Cowper

### Bible Verses to Help You
*And we know that in all things God works for the good of those who love him, who have been called according to his purpose.*
(Romans 8:28)

*Trust in the Lord with all your heart and lean not on your own understanding; in all your ways acknowledge him, and he will make your paths straight.*
(Proverbs 3:5–6)

### Suggested further reading
Proverbs 16:1–9

### Reflect and respond
Accept what has happened, or not happened, and bring your feelings to God knowing that He never disappoints.

# 28

# When Counting the Cost of
## *Discipleship*

Jesus speaks a number of times about the cost of following Him. In Luke 14:27 He says, "Anyone who does not carry his cross and follow me cannot be my disciple". We may find it hard to understand what taking up our cross is all about.

The principle of Jesus taking up His cross was not the burden of it, but the willingness. He laid aside everything else, facing His only objective, that of doing His Father's will. He could say to His Father, "not my will, but yours be done".

Discipleship is always based on an attitude of heart and mind, and the willingness and obedience which follows. We need to consider our position with Jesus, and the depth of commitment we are prepared to make. The more we know and appreciate God's redeeming work in our lives, the simpler taking up our cross can become.

Paul took up his cross from the moment of his amazing encounter with Jesus. He let go of everything both past and personal, in order that he might know God in the deepest relationship possible. His conversion was so life-changing, that knowing God became his consuming passion, it outweighed every other desire in his life, he considered "everything a loss compared to the surpassing greatness of knowing Christ Jesus my Lord" (Philippians 3:8). He counted the cost and decided to stake everything on being a true disciple.

> *It seems amazingly difficult to put on the yoke of Christ, but immediately we do put it on, everything becomes easy.*
> Oswald Chambers

### Bible Verses to Help You

*What is more, I consider everything a loss compared to the surpassing greatness of knowing Christ Jesus my Lord, for whose sake I have lost all things. I consider them rubbish, that I may gain Christ and be found in him, not having a righteousness of my own that comes from the law, but that which is through faith in Christ – the righteousness that comes from God and is by faith.*
*(Philippians 3: 8–9)*

### Suggested further reading

Psalm 130:1–8

### Reflect and respond

Ask yourself how much are you prepared to count the cost of following Jesus.

Taking up our cross is easier if we are not trying to hold on to other things at the same time.

# 29

# When You Need
## *Divine Guidance*

Few Christians have difficulty believing in the personal guidance of God. For the most part our difficulty is not with the fact that God guides but how. Usually God guides along five main routes: through prayerful reading of the Scriptures, through the preaching of God's Word, through reason, through circumstances, and through a strong inner witness. How do these all come together when we are in need of personal guidance?

Some people have found God's guidance while prayerfully reading His Word, as a certain verse is quickened to them. Others have heard His voice through a sermon in church. Still others find the divine will by reasoning an issue through, either by themselves or with a godly friend or counsellor. Circumstances can point the way to God's will also. Things may get chaotic, but often God shakes our circumstances to move us in a different direction.

Then finally there is what some Christians call the way of peace. To find guidance it can help to look at the various options open to you, then picture yourself going down them one by one. On one of these paths a deeper peace may rest. Not a thrill, not pleasure, but peace. This may be the road down which God wants you to travel. Remember, however, it's always good to share all your conclusions about God's guidance, if you can, with a wise and godly friend.

> "Abraham did not know the way, but he knew the Guide."
> *Lee Robertson*

### Bible Verses to Help You
*Trust in the Lord with all your heart and lean not on your own understanding; in all your ways acknowledge him, and he will make your paths straight.*
(Proverbs 3:5–6)

*Your word is a lamp to my feet and a light for my path.*
(Psalm 119:105)

### Suggested further reading
Psalm 25:1–5

### Reflect and respond
What have you done so far to seek God for guidance?

Have you sought Him in His Word and with prayer?

Have you established an "inner witness" that brings peace to your chosen path?

# 30

# When the
# *Storm Rages*

In our day-to-day routines, we may sometimes experience feelings of frustration when we hit a crisis and it seems as though nobody is there to understand. We might even know the sense of fear and anger which the disciples experienced in the boat as the storm raged (Mark 4:35–41).

We need to know God's peace at times like this. In the account of Jesus and His disciples caught in the storm, Jesus demonstrates two kinds of peace, inner peace and outward peace. Both are beyond natural human experience, they are God's supernatural gifts.

When we are caught in our own storm our faith and trust in God needs to extend beyond our natural experience for us to know His supernatural power at work in us. How can we know inner peace? It is a gift of God which we can ask for in simple faith. In John 14:27, when Jesus was about to leave His disciples here on earth, He said to them (and to those who would follow after them), "Peace I leave with you; my peace I give you. I do not give to you as the world gives."

Ask God to give you this inner peace which defies human understanding and comes from the indwelling of his Holy Spirit. This inner peace which Jesus displayed will then give you the strength and confidence to deal with the outward storms of life.

> *"The wise man in the storm prays to God, not for safety from danger, but for deliverance from fear. It is the storm within which endangers him, not the storm without."*
>
> Ralph Waldo Emerson

### Bible Verses to Help You

*He said to his disciples, "Why are you so afraid? Do you still have no faith?"*
*(Mark 4:40)*

*Do not be anxious about anything, but in everything, by prayer and petition, with thanksgiving, present your requests to God. And the peace of God, which transcends all understanding, will guard your hearts and your minds in Christ Jesus.*
*(Philippians 4:6–7)*

### Suggested further reading

Psalm 46:1–3

### Reflect and respond

Do you believe that if Jesus said, "Let us go over to the other side", He would let you sink halfway?

Ask Jesus for His promise of peace to become your experience.

# 31

# When You Feel Forgotten by *God*

It is forgivable, when overtaken by all kinds of difficulties and problems, to think that we are forgotten by God. Forgivable, but not true. From observation and experience it appears that the Christians who fall prey to this misapprehension are those who struggle with a deep sense of inferiority and see themselves as being of little consequence on this earth. Feeling of little importance on earth they deduce, erroneously, they are of little importance in heaven. The psalmist reminds us in Psalm 139 that God's thoughts are always towards us and that they are more in number than the grains of sand (v. 18).

But perhaps the greatest verse we can focus our attention on when tempted to think that God has forgotten us is Isaiah 49:16: "See, I have engraved you on the palms of my hands." The palm of the hand has passed into our proverbs as a symbol of familiarity. We sometimes hear people say: "I know it like the palm of my hand." It is on the palm of His hand, says the prophet Isaiah, that God has put our names. And they are not just written there, but engraved there. This means our names are before Him in such a way that they cannot be overlooked. He does not depend on a ministering spirit to bring our names to His attention. They are imprinted there – on the palms of His hands.

*"God's investment in us is so great he could not possibly abandon us."*
Erwin W. Lutzer.

### Bible Verses to Help You

*"Can a mother forget the baby at her breast and have no compassion on the child she has borne? Though she may forget, I will not forget you!"*
*(Isaiah 49:15)*

### Suggested further reading

Exodus 34:1–7

### Reflect and respond

Have you swallowed the lie of the enemy that God does not care?

Have you sought the security of the Scriptures to see the truc Father?

Bask in the knowledge that God knows you personally.

# 32

# When Facing
# *Redundancy*

Nothing can plunge the soul into a depressed or disconsolate mood more effectively than when one is made redundant or is unemployed. At such times men particularly can feel frustrated, devalued, worthless, and insignificant. The intensity of these feelings will vary, however, depending on whether we draw our sense of worth from what we do or from who we are. If we draw our feelings of worth from the things we do (our job, profession, performance, etc.) then when our circumstances prevent us from contributing as we have done, the usual emotional response is to feel shattered.

The way our emotions react is directly related to the way we perceive and evaluate what has happened to us. This is why one of the most crucial issues to settle in life is the understanding of where our worth truly lies – in who we are or in what we do. What we do in terms of our work is important, but not all-important. The most important thing in life, and the balancing factor in all of life's problems, is to know exactly who we are and where our true worth lies. As Christians our worth lies in the fact that we belong to God, that we are heirs of God and joint heirs with Christ (Romans 8:17). Taking hold of this truth will not stop us from hurting when life becomes difficult but it can mean the difference between being shaken or being shattered.

> *"I have little faith; but it is in a great God."*
> *Kathryn Kuhlman*

## Bible Verses to Help You

*But he said to me, "My grace is sufficient for you, for my power is made perfect in weakness."*
(2 Corinthians 12:9)

*The Lord is my shepherd, I shall not be in want. He makes me lie down in green pastures, he leads me beside quiet waters, he restores my soul. He guides me in paths of righteousness for his name's sake.*
(Psalm 23:1–3)

## Suggested further reading

Ephesians 1:1–6

## Reflect and respond

Have you realised that your security was based in something other than God?

Ask God to forgive you, and to secure your foundations on the Rock.

Praise God that He has made you a joint heir with Jesus.

# 33

# When Caught in
# *Debt*

Sadly, when the unexpected happens financially, very few of us know what to do next. The main reason for this is that we have never been taught about handling money. Most people tend to live up to, or usually just beyond their means, and use credit to enable them to do so. Remarkably, the more we earn the more we borrow. Is it any wonder then that panic sets in when we hit a major reverse?

It is a lack of financial education that often leads us into crisis in the first place. We happily take on commitments, which if we had budgeted we would have known we could not afford. We tend to spend addictively and impulsively, and often significantly underestimate our necessary outgoings. When an unexpected adverse event, such as an interest rise or major car repair occurs, we have no resources to cover it. We also tend to believe what we are told and what we are sold. Many of us don't bother with the small print because we haven't understood the large.

But not only do we need sound practical teaching we

also need sound biblical teaching. The Bible says more about handling money and posses-sions than most other subjects. The world about us shouts "spend, spend, spend", but Jesus quietly asks us to wait and listen and learn from Him. We need to set our eyes on things above and learn to be good stewards of God's resources.

> *"There is nothing wrong with people possessing riches. The wrong comes when riches possess people."*
> Billy Graham

### Bible Verses to Help You

*And my God shall supply all your need according to His riches in glory by Christ Jesus. Now to our God and Father be glory forever and ever. Amen.*
(Philippians 4:19–20 NKJ)

*"Do not store up for yourselves treasures on earth, where moth and rust destroy, and where thieves break in and steal. But store up for yourselves treasures in heaven … For where your treasure is, there your heart will be also.*
(Matthew 6:19–21)

### Suggested further reading

Proverbs 16:19–23

### Reflect and respond

Set your mind that, with God's help, you will straighten out your finances.

Don't be ashamed to seek expert help.

# 34

# When Struggling with
## *Anger*

Even Jesus became angry when a group of critics waited to see if He would heal a man in the synagogue. The Bible says: "He looked round at them in anger and, deeply distressed" (Mark 3:5). His was a righteous anger, for it consisted of grief that some in the congregation preferred Him not to heal because it was the Sabbath.

Unrighteous anger comes about largely from someone or something blocking our goal. Every action we undertake is an attempt to reach a goal that deep down makes good sense to us. When a goal is blocked, depending on how important the goal seems to us, the consequent emotion will be either a feeling of mild frustration or blazing anger. It is harmful to deny we are angry; we should always acknowledge it, and then focus on what is causing the anger.

The way to avoid incapacitating anger is to see that the obstruction of a goal makes no difference to our security in Christ. And we must know, also, the difference between

a desire and a demand. When we simply desire something and it is blocked, we are only
mildly frustrated. When we demand
something, and it is blocked, we
become deeply frustrated. Those
whose confidence is in Christ, rather
than in the good feelings that come
from the achievement of goals, find anger
to be no longer an unmanageable issue.

> *"Hot heads
> and cold hearts
> never solved
> anything."*
> Billy Graham

### Bible Verses to Help You
*Refrain from anger and turn from wrath; do not fret – it
leads only to evil.*
*(Psalm 37:8)*

*"In your anger do not sin": Do not let the sun go
down while you are still angry, and do not give the devil
a foothold.*
*(Ephesians 4:26–27)*

### Suggested further reading
James 1:17–20

### Reflect and respond
Have you identified a problem with unrestrained anger?

Go to God and ask Him to help you to define the difference
between righteous and unrighteous anger.

Set goals based on revelation from the Father – watch
them blossom.

# 35

# When Battling with
# *Sexual Frustration*

The hunger for sex, we must recognise, is no more shameful than the hunger for food. However, this should not be taken to mean that, like the hunger for food, it must be indulged. We can't live without food, but we can live without sex.

The main problem underlying sexual frustration is that of the release of sexual energy. With married people this can be done legitimately through the act of sexual intercourse, but for single people this is forbidden by Scripture. How do single people, and in some circumstances married people also, handle a clamant sex drive? Is masturbation the answer? Scripture is relatively silent on this issue, and some feel that when no other relief can be found, masturbation is permissible, providing no sexual images are being entertained.

There is "a more excellent way", though – the way of sublimation. Sublimation is the rechannelling of energies into another and higher level of activity. One of the best practitioners of this was the apostle Paul. He was creative at the place of the mind and spirit, thus his lower drives were being sublimated.

When all the energies of the spirit are focused on Christ and His kingdom, sexual energies will not be eliminated, but they will be prevented from being a cause of frustration. Many single persons with a strong sex drive have found that it loses its persistent power when they lose themselves in strong service for the Master.

> "The more a man denies himself, the more shall he obtain from God."
> Horace Bushnell

### Bible Verses to Help You

*Therefore, I urge you, brothers, in view of God's mercy, to offer your bodies as living sacrifices, holy and pleasing to God – this is your spiritual act of worship.*
(Romans 12:1)

*Just as you used to offer the parts of your body in slavery to impurity and to ever-increasing wickedness, so now offer them in slavery to righteousness leading to holiness.*
(Romans 6:19)

### Suggested further reading

1 Corinthians 6:18–20

### Reflect and respond

Are your motivations dominated by the flesh?

Have you placed sexual desire in proper context?

Place you energies in wholehearted devotion to God and His kingdom.

# 36

# When God's Promises are *Delayed*

The Scriptures are full of instances of people struggling to make sense of God's delays. Take, for example, Abraham's long wait for a son. Or Joseph's extended years in prison as a victim of cruel circumstances. When something that God has promised is slow in coming to pass, life can become very confusing and perplexing. We look at opportunities that are being missed and cry out: "Why? Why? Why?"

The first thing we should do when faced by a delayed promise is to check that we received a divine promise in the first place and that we are not victims of wishful thinking. Many take words from the Bible which were meant only for certain people in Scripture, apply them to themselves, and then become disappointed when they do not come to pass. So check to see that it was a clear promise God gave you from His Word.

Once you are sure of this then keep in mind that God brings things to pass at precisely the right time. There must be no equivocation on this point, for once we question the fact of God's perfect timing we open

ourselves up to all kind of doubts. We can't stop doubt
entering our heart, of course, but we
can stop it lodging there.
Whatever God has promised
you (and you are sure it is a
promise), then rest assured it
will come to pass. Not always in
your time. But always in His.

> *"Faith takes God
> without any ifs. If God
> says anything, faith says,
> 'I believe it'; faith says,
> 'Amen' to it."*
> D. L. Moody

### Bible Verses to Help You
*For he remembered his holy promise given to his
servant Abraham.*
*(Psalm 105:42)*

*Let us hold unswervingly to the hope we profess, for he
who promised is faithful.*
*(Hebrews 10:23)*

### Suggested further reading
Habakkuk 2:1–3

### Reflect and respond
Are questions over God's timing dominating your life?

Are your sure of God's promises to you?

Trust that the Father has your life in His faithful hands.

# 37

# When Your Love for the Lord Begins to *Wane*

It should always cause us great concern when our love for the Lord Jesus Christ diminishes and wanes. Our love for Christ, we must always remember, is a response to His love for us. "We love because he first loved us", says the apostle John in 1 John 4:19. Our souls are designed to respond to divine love, not manufacture it. When we focus on how much we are loved by Him, and allow ourselves to be impacted by that fact, it will inevitably create a response in us. However, it must be emphasised that this principle will only work when sin has been put out of our hearts. In Revelation 2:4 our Lord says to the church in Ephesus: "I have this against you, that you have left your first love" (NKJ). Note they had not lost their love, but left it. There is a great difference between losing something and leaving it. We leave our love for Christ when we violate one or more of His commandments, and love cannot be recovered until sin is confessed and God's forgiveness sought.

Once all is dealt with then the principle mentioned above should be followed – focus not so much on how you can love Him but on His love for you. Gaze on the cross, see love bleeding for you. The greater your awareness of how much you are loved, the greater will be your response.

> "I love, my God, but with no love of mine,
> For I have none to give;
> I love thee, Lord, but all the love is thine,
> For by thy love I live."
>
> *Jeanne Marie*
> *de la Mothe Guyon*

### Bible Verses to Help You

*How great is the love the Father has lavished on us, that we should be called children of God! And that is what we are!*
(1 John 3:1)

*What, then, shall we say in response to this? If God is for us, who can be against us? He who did not spare his own Son, but gave him up for us all – how will he not also, along with him, graciously give us all things?*
(Romans 8:31–32)

### Suggested further reading

Ephesians 3:17–19

### Reflect and respond

Identify any areas of your life that have cooled between God and you.

Look to the cross afresh, and meditate on His love for you.

# 38

# When Marriage
## *Fails*

The break-up of a marriage can be more traumatic and painful than even the death of one's partner. In death one says "goodbye", and after a period of grief and mourning the heart gathers new strength and feels alive once again. But a separation or divorce takes a toll that is hard to describe. Friends can help and be a great support, but there is no one who understands like Jesus. He knows, more than anyone, what it means to be rejected, misunderstood, and hurt.

First we must talk to God about the matter. It is vitally important to acknowledge to yourself and to God all your hurt or angry feelings. Next, search the Scriptures daily, asking God to give you words of encouragement. God quickens different Scriptures to different people. The Psalms can be of special help in this connection. Third, come to terms, painful though it may be, with the fact your marriage may not be restored. If there is hope that it may then live in that hope, but also in the knowledge that it may not.

Fourth, remind yourself that you are first a person

before being a partner. Though a partnership may be broken your identity as a person in Christ cannot. Fifth, develop a close and continuing relationship with God in prayer. Being bereft of a partner brings a certain loneliness, but it provides an opportunity for knowing God in a way you might never have known Him before.

> *"Man is born broken. He lives by mending. The grace of God is glue."*
> Eugene Gladstone O'Neil

### Bible Verses to Help You

*My soul finds rest in God alone; my salvation comes from him. He alone is my rock and my salvation; he is my fortress, I will never be shaken.*
(Psalm 62:1–2)

*The Lord is faithful to all his promises and loving towards all he has made. The Lord upholds all those who fall and lifts up all who are bowed down.*
(Psalm 145:13–14)

### Suggested further reading
Nehemiah 1:4 and Matthew 6:15

### Reflect and respond
Is Jesus at the centre of your pain?

Have you talked over with God how you feel?

See this as an opportunity to draw closer to the Father.

# 39

# When Someone Close to You *Dies*

Sooner or later almost every one of us has to face the death of a person we love. Forgive the personal reference here, but some years ago I lost my wife through cancer and I know what I am about to say is true.

When death takes from our side someone we love, the pain we experience can, at times, be almost intolerable. We must not be afraid to express our feelings to God whatever they may be – anger, frustration, fear, hurt, and so on. These feelings are better expressed than repressed. C. S. Lewis said that when his wife died he railed against God for a while. Then, when he had spent himself in accusations against the Almighty, he sensed the loving arms of God go around him in a way that even he was unable to describe. God is not upset with us when we tell Him exactly how we feel, He listens, feels for us, and understands. As soon as possible, though, we must invite Him into our pain and draw upon His comforting strength and support.

Divine comfort does not mean that our tears will dry

up, or our grief come to a sudden halt. These are natural processes that have a powerful therapeutic effect. What it does mean is that we will feel God there in the midst of our tears and grief. The pain must be entered into and worked through – even the pain of saying "goodbye".

> *"To weep is to make less the depth of grief."*
> William Shakespeare

### Bible Verses to Help You

*Blessed are those who mourn, for they will be comforted.*
*(Matthew 5:4)*

*Remember your word to your servant, for you have given me hope. My comfort in my suffering is this: Your promise preserves my life.*
*(Psalm 119:49–50)*

### Suggested further reading

Psalm 23:1–4

### Reflect and respond

Have you acknowledged your pain to God?

Understand that the mourning process is healthy and needed.

Allow the tears to act as divine therapy – draw close to God.

# 40

# When Sick and Tired of Being
## *Sick and Tired*

Clearly, the Scriptures reveal that God is able and willing to heal the sicknesses of His people. He healed men and women in Old Testament times, and in New Testament times too. When serious sickness afflicts us we ought to seek all legitimate means of healing, beginning first with inviting those who represent the local church to pray over us, anointing us with oil (James 5:14). Also, it is not lack of faith to seek medical help when sick – even when one has been prayed for by the leaders of the church.

But what happens when sickness continues and healing does not come? God is able to keep us brave when not blithe; aware of His presence even though not abounding with vitality. God does not always heal, and no matter how we may rationalise this fact we must see there is an element of mystery about the subject of healing. No one knew or has ever been more conscious of the problem of why God does not always deliver us from our afflictions than God's servant Job. He asked numerous questions of the Almighty but none of them, in fact, was answered. Instead God gave Job something better – a richer and deeper sense of His presence.

God may not give us a clear answer as to why we are not healed but He will, if we let Him, give us a richer awareness of Himself. Nothing can be more wonderful than that.

> "God whispers to us in our pleasures, speaks in our conscience, but shouts in our pains: it is his megaphone to rouse a deaf world."
>
> C.S. Lewis

### Bible Verses to Help You

*Praise the Lord, O my soul; all my inmost being, praise his holy name. Praise the Lord, O my soul, and forget not all his benefits – who forgives all your sins and heals all your diseases …*
*(Psalm 103:1–3)*

*… do not fear, for I am with you; do not be dismayed, for I am your God. I will strengthen you and help you; I will uphold you with my righteous right hand.*
*(Isaiah 41:10)*

### Suggested further reading

Matthew 8:16–17

### Reflect and respond

Have you asked the leaders in your church to pray for you?

Have you taken the practical medical steps that are necessary?

Dig deep to feel the loving arms of the great Healer – Jesus.

# Content Source Material

Sections 1, 3, 5, 7, 9, 11, 13, 15, 17, 19 and 26
are taken from:
Dr Bill & Frances Munro, *A Place of Rest*,
CWR, 1996.

Sections 2, 4, 6, 8, 10, 12, 14, 16, 18, 20, 22, 25, 27, 29,
31–32, 34–40 are taken from:
Selwyn Hughes, *Your Personal Encourager*,
CWR, 1994.

Sections 21, 28 and 30 are taken from:
Hilary Vogel, *Strength to Care*,
CWR, 1996.

Sections 23–24 are taken from:
David & Maureen Brown, *Breakthrough to Love*,
CWR, 1996.

Section 33 is taken from:
Keith Tondeur, *Facing up to Financial Crisis*,
CWR, 1995.


All these titles available from CWR
(see following pages for details).

NATIONAL DISTRIBUTORS

UK: (and countries not listed below)

CWR, PO Box 230, Farnham, Surrey GU9 8XG.

Tel: (01252) 784710 Outside UK (44) 1252 784710

**AUSTRALIA:** CMC Australasia, PO Box 519, Belmont, Victoria 3216.
Tel: (03) 5241 3288

**CANADA:** CMC Distribution Ltd, PO Box 7000, Niagara on the Lake,
Ontario L0S 1J0.
Tel: (0800) 325 1297

**GHANA:** Challenge Enterprises of Ghana, PO Box 5723, Accra.
Tel: (021) 222437/223249 Fax: (021) 226227

**HONG KONG:** Cross Communications Ltd, 1/F,
562A Nathan Road, Kowloon.
Tel: 2780 1188 Fax: 2770 6229

**INDIA:** Crystal Communications, 10-3-18/4/1, East Marredpally,
Secunderabad – 500 026.
Tel/Fax: (040) 7732801

**KENYA:** Keswick Bookshop, PO Box 10242, Nairobi.
Tel: (02) 331692/226047

**MALAYSIA:** Salvation Book Centre (M) Sdn Bhd, 23 Jalan SS 2/64,
47300 Petaling Jaya, Selangor.
Tel: (03) 78766411/78766797
Fax: (03) 78757066/78756360

**NEW ZEALAND:** CMC New Zealand Ltd, Private Bag,
17910 Green Lane, Auckland.
Tel: (09) 5249393 Fax: (09) 5222137

**NIGERIA:** FBFM, Helen Baugh House, 96 St Finbarr's College Road, Akoka, Lagos.
Tel: (01) 7747429/4700218/825775/827264

**PHILIPPINES:** OMF Literature Inc, 776 Boni Avenue, Mandaluyong City.
Tel: (02) 531 2183 Fax: (02) 531 1960

**REPUBLIC OF IRELAND:** Scripture Union, 40 Talbot Street, Dublin 1.
Tel: (01) 8363764

**SINGAPORE:** Campus Crusade Asia Ltd, 315 Outram Road, 06-08 Tan Boon Liat Building, Singapore 169074.
Tel: (065) 222 3640

**SOUTH AFRICA:** Struik Christian Books, 80 MacKenzie Street, PO Box 1144, Cape Town 8000.
Tel: (021) 462 4360 Fax: (021) 461 3612

**SRI LANKA:** Christombu Books, 27 Hospital Street, Colombo 1.
Tel: (01) 433142/328909

**TANZANIA:** CLC Christian Book Centre, PO Box 1384, Mkwepu Street, Dar es Salaam.
Tel: (051) 2119439

**UGANDA:** New Day Bookshop, PO Box 2021, Kampala.
Tel: (041) 255377

**ZIMBABWE:** Word of Life Books, Shop 4, Memorial Building, 35 S Machel Avenue, Harare.
Tel: (04) 781305 Fax: (04) 774739

For e-mail addresses, visit the CWR web site: www.cwr.org.uk

ISBN 1 85345 1789

ISBN 1 85345 1797

ISBN 1 85345 1770

ISBN 1 85345 1800

This new *Pocket Encourager* series offers biblical help, guidance and encouragement for everyone. Each title explores various aspects of the Christian experience, such as relationships, Bible study and coping with responsibility. Great gifts!

**£3.99** each

*Cover to Cover* and *Cover to Cover – God's People* are exciting annual reading plans available in 6 partworks with their own attractive case, or as a softback book. *Cover to Cover* is now also available in hardback.

**Cover to Cover**

*Cover to Cover* explores God's Word chronologically, taking in the events of history as they happened with charts, maps, illustrations, diagrams and a helpful time line that places the Bible in a historical context.

**Cover to Cover – God's People**

*Cover to Cover – God's People* profiles 58 of the Bible's most fascinating and instructive personalities, helping you to learn invaluable lessons from these men and women of Scripture.

| | |
|---|---|
| Softback and partworks | **£9.95** |
| Cover to Cover hardback | **£12.95** |

These inspiring devotionals contain six, specially selected themes from *Every Day with Jesus* that will nourish your soul and stimulate your faith. Each book contains 365 undated daily readings, prayers, further study questions and a topical index.

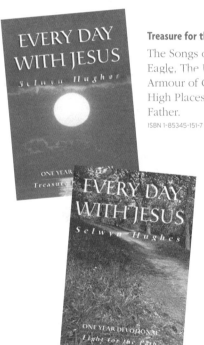

### Treasure for the Heart

The Songs of Ascents, The Divine Eagle, The Lord's Prayer, The Armour of God, Hind's Feet on High Places, Your Father and My Father.
ISBN 1-85345-151-7

### Light for the Path

The Uniqueness of our Faith, The Search for Meaning, The Twenty-third Psalm, The Spirit-filled Life, Strong at the Broken Places, Going Deeper with God.
ISBN 1-85345-134-7

### A Fresh Vision of God

The Vision of God, From Confusion to
Confidence, The Beatitudes, The Power of a New
Perspective, The Corn of Wheat Afraid to Die,
Heaven-sent Revival.

ISBN 1-85345-121-5

### Water for the Soul

Staying Spiritually Fresh,
Rebuilding Broken Walls,
The Character of God,
When Sovereignty Surprises,
The Fruit of the Spirit,
Seven Pillars of Wisdom.

ISBN 1-85345-128-2

**£5.99** each

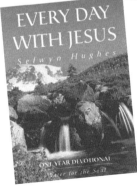

What would Christ have to say about our modern-day problems? "He would give the same answers that He gave us in His Word", says *Every Day with Jesus* author, Selwyn Hughes.

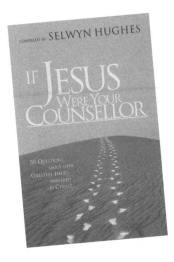

**£6.95**

Softback, 280 pages
198 x 130mm

*If Jesus were your Counsellor* offers 50 biblical answers to questions about faith and life. Selwyn Hughes brings more than four decades of counselling experience to this easy to follow and beautifully designed book, which recognises that Scripture always holds the answer.

*If Jesus were your Counsellor* uses *The Message* translation of the New Testament, making it contemporary and easy to understand, and the book-mark extensions to the cover provide a simple and effective way to keep your place as you read Christ's response to issues such as love, loneliness, relationships, guilt and belief.

*Let Jesus be your Counsellor*

The Discipleship Series combines practical advice with biblical principles to bring you invaluable insights into your faith in Jesus and growing with Him. Each title considers some of the most vital aspects of Christian living, such as marriage, prayer, and the Church. Essential reading!

### 10 Principles for a Happy Marriage

- Engaging approach to marriage God's way
- Healthy marriage check list
- Practical advice and help

### 15 Ways to a More Effective Prayer Life

- Revolutionise your prayer life
- Flexible suggestions for the individual
- Considers different personalities and lifestyles

### 5 Insights to Discovering Your Place in the Body of Christ

- Understanding the gifts in Scripture
- Discovering your ministry
- Developing your gift

**£3.95** each